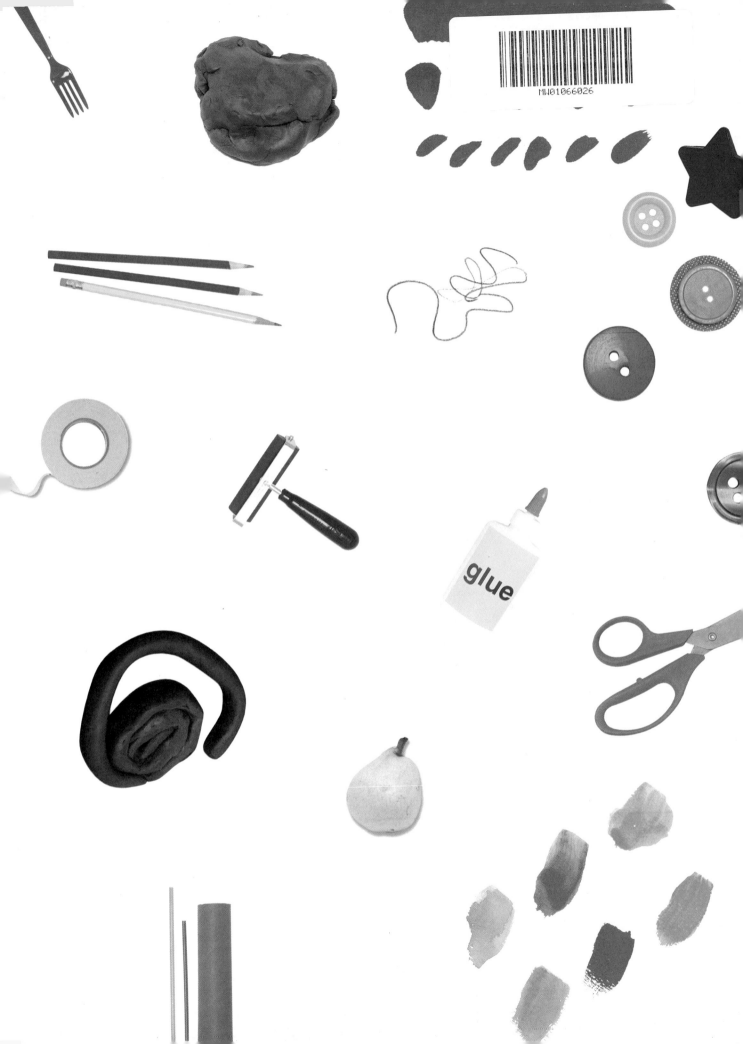

glue

MW01066026

ART Express

AUTHORS

Vesta A. H. Daniel

Lee Hanson

Kristen Pederson Marstaller

Susana R. Monteverde

Harcourt Brace & Company

Orlando   Atlanta   Austin   Boston   San Francisco   Chicago   Dallas   New York   Toronto   London

http://www.hbschool.com

For permission to reprint copyrighted material, grateful acknowledgment is made to the following sources:

Gryphon House, Inc., Beltsville, Maryland 20704-0207: "I Rarely Have Soup" from *Move Over, Mother Goose!* by Ruth I. Dowell. Text copyright © 1987 by Ruth I. Dowell.

HarperCollins Publishers: From "Rudolph Is Tired of the City" in *Bronzeville Boys and Girls* by Gwendolyn Brooks. Text copyright © 1956 by Gwendolyn Brooks Blakely.

Philomel Books: From *Draw Me a Star* by Eric Carle. Copyright © 1992 by Eric Carle.

Talking Stone Press, Boston: From "Family Gifts" by Judith Steinbergh and Victor Cockburn in *Where I Come From! Songs and Poems from Many Cultures.* Text © 1991 by Judith Steinbergh and Victor Cockburn.

Wonderland Music Publishing Company, Inc.: "Step in Time" by Richard M. Sherman and Robert B. Sherman. Lyrics copyright © 1963 by Wonderland Music Company, Inc; copyright renewed.

Dear Boys and Girls,

You have been making art for a long time. Maybe you have used crayons, paint, or things you found outdoors. You have seen art every day—in your home, on TV, or around your town.

The art inside this book was made by people all over the world. Some was made by children. Get ready to look at art, think about art, and make your own art!

Sincerely,
The Authors

C O N T E N T S

To the Student ● 3

Looking at Art ● 10

Keeping a Sketchbook ● 12

 **UNIT 1** **Start with Art** ● 14

LESSON **1** What Is Art? 16
A BIG PICTURE

LESSON **2** Looking at Animals 18
ANIMAL DRAWING

CONNECTIONS Visiting a Museum 20
ART AND CULTURE

LESSON **3** Tasty Art 22
FOOD PICTURE

LESSON **4** What Do You Hear? 24
DRAWING SOUNDS

CONNECTIONS Murals 26
COMMUNITY ART

LESSON **5** What Do You See? 28
BRUSHSTROKES

LESSON **6** Art You Can Feel 30
ASSEMBLAGE

REFLECTING AND REVIEWING 32

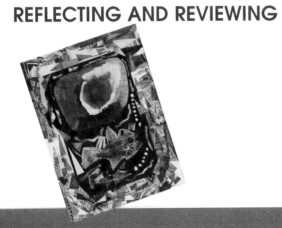

 **UNIT 2** **Inside Art.** 34

LESSON **7** Kinds of Lines 36
LINE DRAWING

LESSON **8** Lines Make Shapes 38
SHAPE PICTURE

CONNECTIONS Toy Maker 40
CAREERS IN ART

LESSON **9** Find the Patterns 42
PATTERN PRINTS

LESSON **10** Mixing Colors 44
ANIMAL PAINTING

CONNECTIONS Art Around You 46
EVERYDAY ART

LESSON **11** Textures All Around 48
CRAYON RUBBINGS

LESSON **12** I Paint Me 50
SELF-PORTRAIT

REFLECTING AND REVIEWING 52

5

UNIT 3 **Art All Around** • 54

LESSON **13** Colors and Patterns 56
DRAWING PATTERNS

LESSON **14** Masks 58
ANIMAL MASK

CONNECTIONS Lois Ehlert's Art 60
ART AND LITERATURE

LESSON **15** Warm and Cool Colors 62
PAINTING A PLACE

LESSON **16** What Is a Landscape? 64
LANDSCAPE

CONNECTIONS Tiny Works of Art 66
EVERYDAY ART

LESSON **17** Beautiful Animals 68
MODELING FORMS

LESSON **18** Looking Closely 70
DETAILED DRAWING

REFLECTING AND REVIEWING 72

UNIT 4 **Outside Art** • 74

LESSON 19 Collage Scenes .76
COLLAGE

LESSON 20 Cityscapes .78
CITYSCAPE PAINTING

CONNECTIONS Kwanzaa Playground 80
COMMUNITY ART

LESSON 21 Light and Dark Colors 82
CHANGING COLORS

LESSON 22 Seascapes .84
SEASCAPE PAINTING

CONNECTIONS Marc Brown .86
ART AND LITERATURE

LESSON 23 Monoprints to Share 88
MONOPRINT

LESSON 24 Textures in Clay 90
CLAY IMPRINTS

REFLECTING AND REVIEWING 92

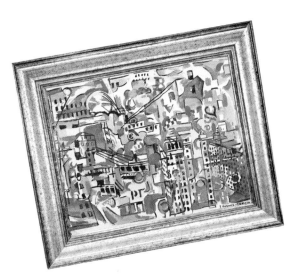

UNIT 5 Artful Celebrations . 94

LESSON 25 Surprising Sculptures 96
USING FOUND OBJECTS

LESSON 26 Sculptures of People 98
CLAY FIGURES

CONNECTIONS Photographer: Flor Garduño 100
CAREERS IN ART

LESSON 27 Still Life 102
STILL-LIFE DRAWING

LESSON 28 Quilts 104
CLASS QUILT

CONNECTIONS Parades 106
CELEBRATION ART

LESSON 29 Flags for All 108
SCHOOL FLAG

LESSON 30 American Buildings 110
MODEL BUILDING

REFLECTING AND REVIEWING 112

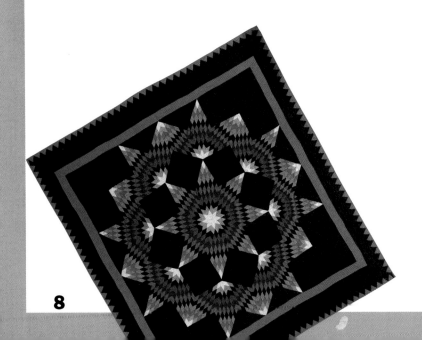

UNIT 6 # The World of Art • 114

LESSON 31 Playful Puppets 116
SOCK PUPPET

LESSON 32 Mosaics 118
PAPER MOSAIC

CONNECTIONS Piñatas 120
CELEBRATION ART

LESSON 33 Clothing 122
PAPER VEST

LESSON 34 Jewelry 124
JEWELRY

CONNECTIONS Kites 126
ART AND CULTURE

LESSON 35 Paper Folding 128
PAPER FLOWERS

LESSON 36 Weaving 130
WEAVING

REFLECTING AND REVIEWING 132

Art Safety • 134
Elements and Principles of Design • 136
Gallery of Artists • 150
Glossary • 160
Index of Artists and Artworks • 170
Index • 172

LOOKING AT ART

Follow these steps when you look at art.

1. Take time to look.

2. Think about what the artist wants you to know.

3. Ask yourself questions.

4. Talk to other people. Find out what they think. Tell them what you think.

What does the artist want you to see?

KEEPING A
SKETCHBOOK

Artists sketch what they see.
They draw in a **sketchbook**.

Sketches of Peter Rabbit and Benjamin Bunny by Beatrix Potter

Illustration from *The Tale of Benjamin Bunny*
by Beatrix Potter

Student Sketch

Make a sketchbook.
Keep your ideas in it.

From *Draw Me a Star* by Eric Carle, 1992

Start with Art

Draw us a cloud,

said the flowers.

And the artist drew clouds

heavy with rain.

— **Eric Carle**
from *Draw Me a Star*

ABOUT ERIC CARLE

Eric Carle has written and
illustrated more than 50
children's picture books.
The Very Hungry Caterpillar
and *The Very Busy Spider*
are two of his books.

What Is Art?

How are these pictures the same?

A *The Lawrence Tree*
by Georgia O'Keeffe, 1929

Artists often show things in new ways. How would you draw a tree to show it in a new way?

> **Where was this artist standing?**

16

B *The Tree*
by Amos Ferguson, 1988

In the Studio

Make a big drawing of a tree. Show it in a new way.

Looking at Animals

Which of these animals would feel soft? Which would feel rough? Artists often try to show how something feels.

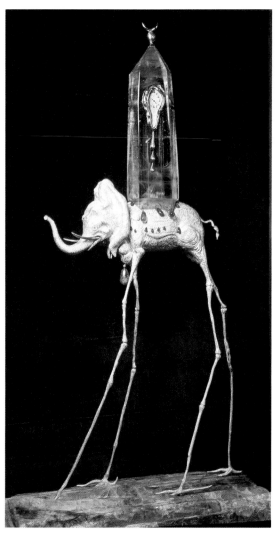

 The Space Elephant by Salvador Dalí, 1961

 The Hare by Albrecht Dürer, 1502

In the Studio

Draw an animal.

1. Sketch animals in your sketchbook.

2. Choose one to draw.

3. Show how the animal would feel if you could touch it.

CONNECTIONS ART AND CULTURE

VISITING A

What are these children doing?

You can see real art in an art museum.

MUSEUM

In a museum, walk slowly.
Talk quietly.

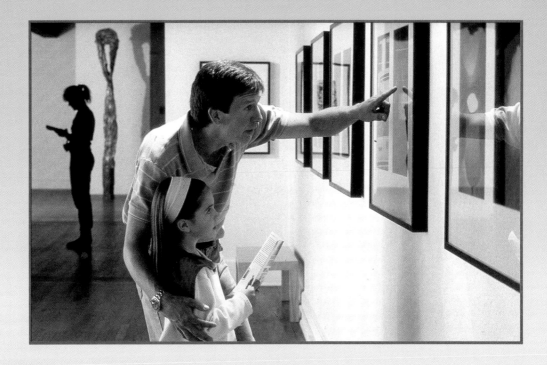

WHAT
DO
YOU
THINK
?

▶ Why is it important to know the rules in an art museum?

Tasty Art

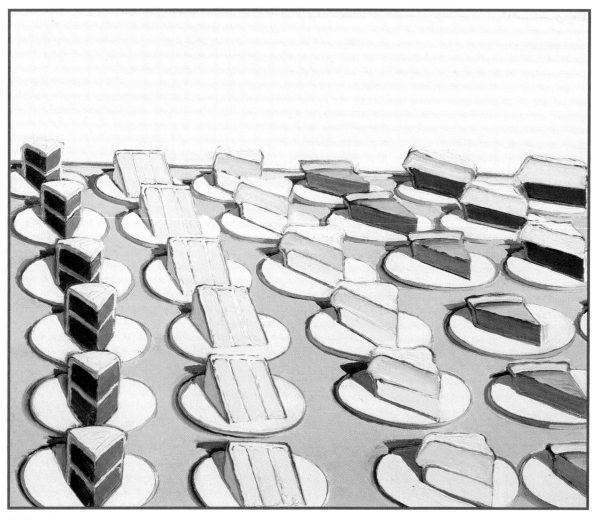

Pie Counter
by Wayne Thiebaud, 1963

How do you think these pies and cakes would taste? How would they smell? Artists help us use all our senses to enjoy art.

Yum! I can almost taste this.

In the Studio

Make a food picture.

1. Cut out pictures of foods that taste and smell good.

2. Group your foods to make a picture. Then glue them.

3. Tell about the tastes and smells in your picture.

What Do You HEAR?

Some pictures make us think of sounds. Which place looks quiet? Which place looks noisy? What would you hear in each picture?

A *Looking along Broadway towards Grace Church* by Red Grooms, 1981

Rooms by the Sea
by Edward Hopper, 1951

In the Studio

Draw a picture of a quiet place or a noisy place.

You can use many colors.

This large painting is called
a mural. It was painted in a
school by children.

If you were in this
mural, what would
you hear?

WHAT
DO
YOU
THINK
?

▶ Think about where you live.

Where would you paint a mural?

What would you paint?

What Do You See?

Sometimes artists want us to use our imaginations. With a classmate, look for things in each picture. Talk about how the artists made the different lines and shapes.

 Around the Circle
by Wassily Kandinsky, 1940

In the Studio

Use a paintbrush in different ways. Make many kinds of lines and shapes.

Clean your brush before using a new color.

Art You Can Feel

What things did the artist use to make this artwork? If you could touch it, how would the different parts feel?

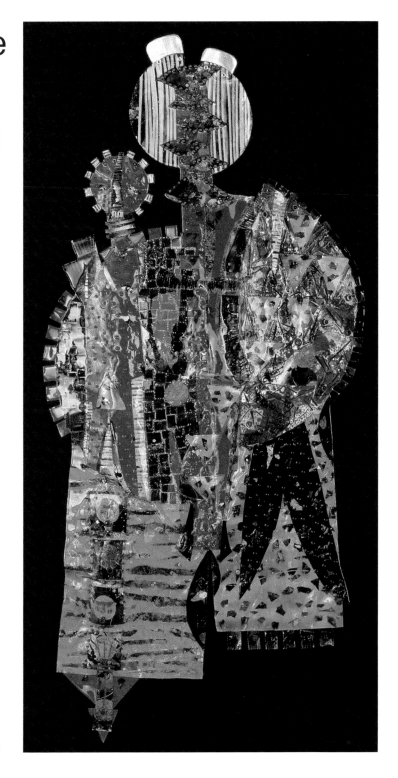

Mother and Child
by Gilda Edwards, 1993

30

In the Studio

Make an assemblage.

1. Find things you like to touch.

2. Glue them to heavy paper.

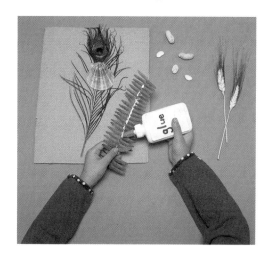

3. Share your artwork. Tell why you chose each thing.

Three Musicians by Pablo Picasso, 1921

Explain why this picture might make you want to sing or dance.

Making Tamales/La Tamalada by Carmen Lomas Garza, 1987

Inside Art

The Very Nicest Place

The fish lives in the brook,

The bird lives in the tree,

But home's the very nicest place

For a little child like me.

—Anonymous

ABOUT CARMEN LOMAS GARZA

Carmen Lomas Garza paints pictures of her family. As a young girl, she dreamed of being an artist. Her family helped her become one.

Self Portrait
by Carmen Lomas Garza, 1980

Kinds of Lines

Look at these pictures. Where do you see **lines**?

Red Interior, Still-life on a Blue Table
by Henri Matisse, 1947

Lines can be straight, curved, and zigzag. Tell how the artist used lines to show his ideas.

In the Studio

Draw a picture using many kinds of lines.

1. Draw a border around your paper. Use different kinds of lines.

2. Draw a picture in the middle of your paper. Use the same kinds of lines that are in your border.

Lines Make Shapes

How are these artworks the same?

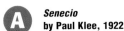

A *Senecio*
by Paul Klee, 1922

B *Le Griffu*
by Germaine Richier, 1952

Do you see lines and shapes,
such as circles or triangles?
Or do you see people?

In the Studio

Make a shape picture.

1. Bend pipe cleaners to make shapes.

2. Glue the shapes onto paper.

3. Draw more shapes to finish your picture.

Use only as much glue as you need.

TOY

This man makes toys. Look at the pictures. Tell how one of his toys is made.

MAKER

PUDDLE JUMPER

DIRT KING

WHAT
DO
YOU
THINK
?

▶ **If you could be a toy maker, what kind of toy would you make?**

Find the Patterns

What lines, shapes, and colors do you see again and again? Repeated parts make **patterns**. How do your eyes move as you look at the patterns in each picture?

A Student artwork

B *Vaudeville*
by Jacob Lawrence, 1951–52

In the Studio

Make a printed pattern.

1. **Dip an object in paint.**

2. **Press the object on paper. Begin a pattern.**

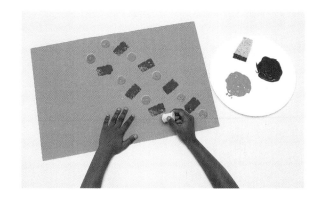

3. **Use different objects and colors to finish the pattern.**

MIXING COLORS

Die grossen blauen Pferde (The Large Blue Horses)
by Franz Marc, 1911

What is different about these horses?
The artist has chosen unusual colors
to show his feelings about them. What
other colors do you see?

A color wheel shows some colors you can make.

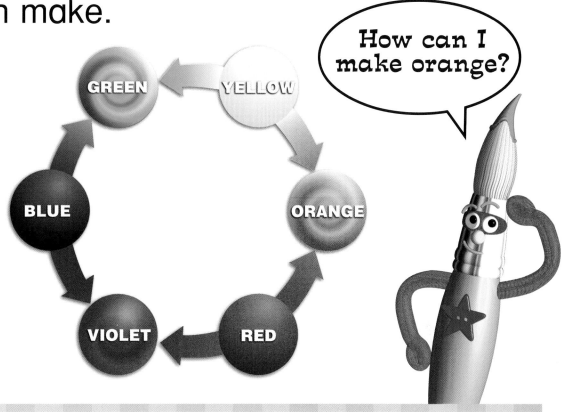

How can I make orange?

In the Studio

Paint a picture of an animal you would like as a pet. Mix two colors to make the color you want.

Art Around

An artist took these pictures. What things do you see?

photograph from *Shapes, Shapes, Shapes* by Tana Hoban

Take a closer look. What shapes and colors can you find?

You

Tell about the shapes and colors in these pictures.

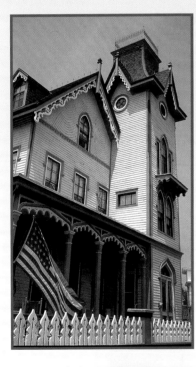

WHAT DO YOU THINK?

▶ Why do you think the artist chose these things for her pictures?

What shapes and colors do you see around you?

47

TEXTURES
All Around

What would each of these things feel like if you could touch it? The way a thing feels is called **texture**. How did this artist show texture?

Flowers, Apple & Pear on a Table, July, 1986
by David Hockney

In the Studio

Make crayon rubbings.

1. Make a design
with shapes.
Glue the shapes
to paper.

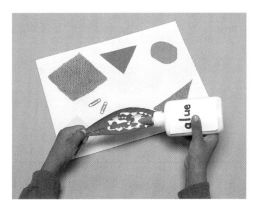

2. Let the glue dry.
Then lay paper
over your design.

3. Rub the side of a
crayon across
the paper.

I Paint Me

A **Self-portrait**
by Marie-Louise-Élisabeth Vigée-Lebrun, 1790

B **Self Portrait**
by Malvin Gray Johnson, 1934

These paintings are both **self-portraits**. Self-portraits are artists' pictures of themselves. What can you tell about these artists from their pictures?

In the Studio

Paint a self-portrait.

1. Look at yourself in a mirror.

2. Paint what you see.

3. Add something you like.

51

Thanksgiving by Doris Lee, 1935

Why is this a good song for this painting? Would you like to get together with these people? Why?

Hoosick Valley (from the Window) by Grandma Moses, 1946

UNIT 3

Art All Around

from _Rudolph Is Tired of the City_

These buildings are too close to me,

I'd like to PUSH away.

I'd like to live in the country,

And spread my arms all day.

—Gwendolyn Brooks

ABOUT GRANDMA MOSES

Grandma Moses's real name was Anna Mary Robertson Moses. She liked to draw and paint as a child. She didn't become a famous artist until she was more than 75 years old!

Colors and Patterns

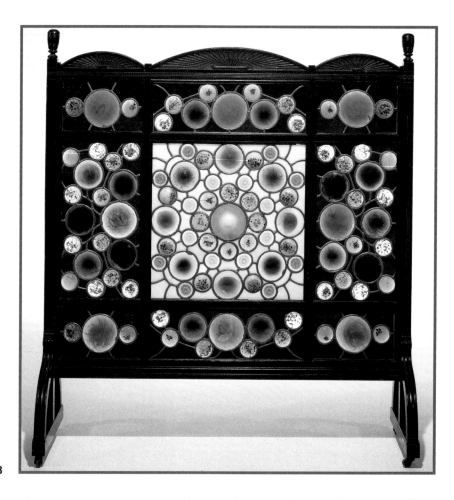

A *Nine-Paneled Firescreen*
by John La Farge, about 1883

What pattern do you see in the feathers?
What colors and shapes create patterns
in pictures **A** and **B**? Patterns help artists
create **unity**. An artwork has unity when
all parts look as if they belong together.

56

B *Peacocks and Peonies I* (detail)
by John La Farge, 1882

In the Studio

**Look for patterns around you.
With markers, draw a new pattern.
Repeat colors and lines.**

What patterns do I see?

Masks

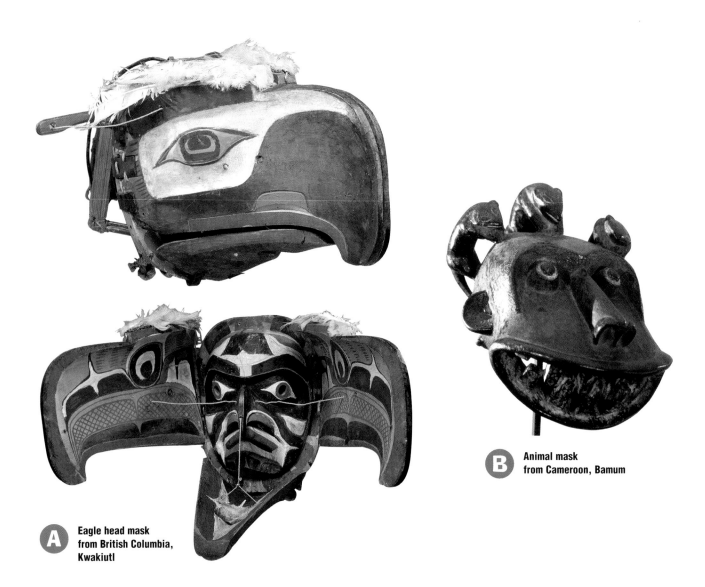

B Animal mask
from Cameroon, Bamum

A Eagle head mask
from British Columbia,
Kwakiutl

How are these masks alike? **Masks** are
a kind of artwork that covers the face.
When a mask is the same on both
sides, it shows **balance**.

In the Studio

Make an animal mask.

1. Draw and cut out two eyes.

2. Make the rest of the face. Keep the balance!

3. Add color and details. Share your mask with others.

LOIS EHLERT'S ART

Lois Ehlert has made pictures for many children's books. What did she use to make this art for a book called *Snowballs*?

60

from *Snowballs*
by Lois Ehlert

WHAT
DO
YOU
THINK
?

▶ **Why did this artist use everyday objects in her pictures? What other things could she have used?**

Warm and Cool Colors

A *From the Plains II*
by Georgia O'Keeffe, 1954

I feel warm.

Which painting shows a warm place? Which shows a cool place? The colors can help you decide. Red and yellow are called warm colors. Blue and green are called cool colors.

B *The Northern Entrance to Orient Bay, Lake Nipigon*
by George Agnew Reid, 1929

In the Studio

Paint a picture of a warm place or a cool place. Use warm or cool colors.

Lesson **16**
LANDSCAPE

What Is a Landscape?

Tell a story about one of these places.

A *Day at the Beach*
by Anna Belle Lee Washington

B Student artwork

These paintings are **landscapes**. A landscape is a picture of a large outdoor space. Where do the land and the sky meet in picture **A**? This line is called the **horizon line**.

64

In the Studio

Paint or draw a landscape.

1. Think of an outdoor space.

2. Draw a horizon line on your paper.

3. Fill in the sky and the land. Add animals, people, or other things that live there.

TINY WORKS

These stamps show things in nature. They remind us about beauty we can see every day.

OF ART

How can you see art every day? Just look at the stamp on a letter! Every stamp is a tiny work of art.

WHAT DO **YOU** THINK ?

▶ If you could make a stamp, what would you show?

Beautiful Animals

How do these animals look different from real ones you have seen?

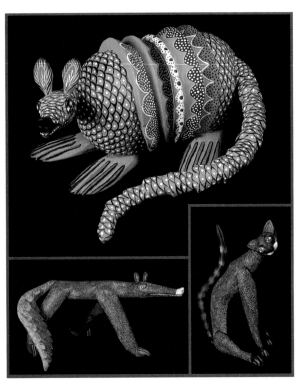

A *Zoo Animals* by Zeny Fuentes

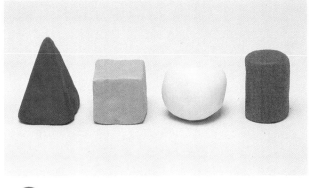

B

Which one has six sides?

Picture **B** shows some **forms**. You can see forms from all sides. What forms do you see in the animals in picture **A**?

68

In the Studio

Make forms with clay.

1. Soften the clay with your hands.

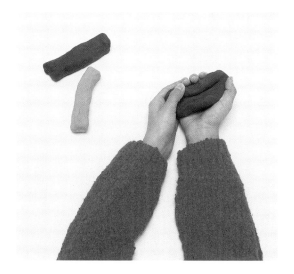

2. Model the clay into different forms.

3. Try making unusual forms.

Looking Closely

Why do you think the artist painted this picture close up?

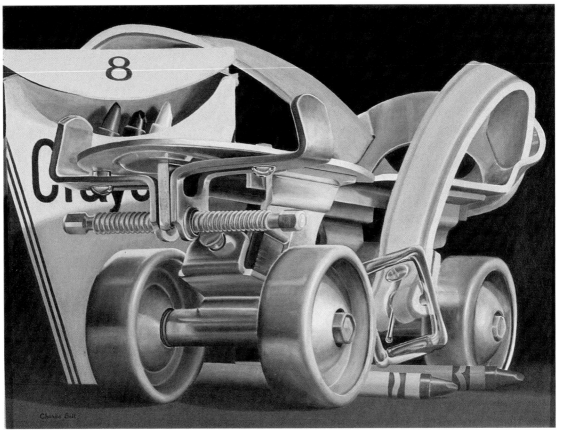

Skate by Charles Bell, 1971

An artist must look at the details, or small parts, of something before painting it. What details do you see?

In the Studio

Draw a close-up picture with details.

1. Look closely at something you see every day.

2. Draw a close-up of what you see. Fill your paper.

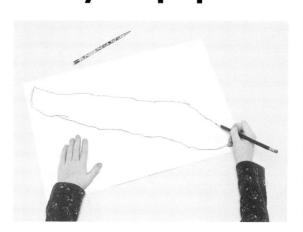

3. Add details and color.

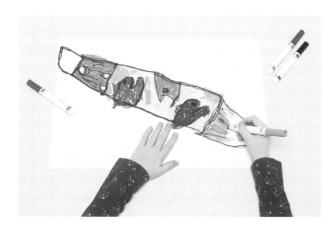

Autumn Leaves, Lake George, N.Y. by Georgia O'Keeffe, 1924

How did the artist make these leaves look real?

Exotic Landscape by Henri Rousseau, 1910

Outside Art

Three Little Monkeys

I know something I won't tell—
Three little monkeys in a peanut
*   shell!*
One can sing and one can dance,
And one can make a pair of pants.

—Anonymous

ABOUT HENRI ROUSSEAU

Henri Rousseau is remembered for his landscapes of jungles and deserts. He visited the zoo to study animals from around the world.

Collage Scenes

Jazz Village by Romare Bearden

This artist made a **collage**. He cut out pictures and grouped them to make his design. He used different colors, textures, and patterns for **variety**. Variety makes artwork more interesting.

In the Studio

Make a collage.

1. Draw a picture of a place. Put people in it.

2. Cut out magazine pictures and glue them to parts of your artwork.

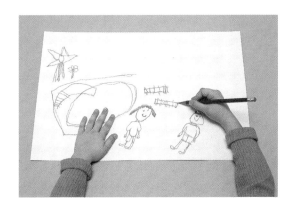

3. Find ways to add variety.

Lesson
20
CITYSCAPE PAINTING

Cityscapes

Look at all the lines!

A *Untitled* by Byron Gin

How are these two artworks the same? How are they different? Artists find their own ways to show big, busy cities. How does each artist make things look as if they are moving?

78

B *New York City–Bird's Eye View*
by Joaquín Torres-García, about 1920

In the Studio

Make a cityscape.
Have something in
your picture look
as if it is moving.

79

Kwanzaa

Barbara Chavous

Shirley Bowen

Queen Brooks

Larry Winston Collins

African Tell-A-Story Board
designed by Shirley Bowen and
created by Larry Winston Collins

These artists wanted children to know about Africa. They made a special place for children to play and learn. Which piece would you like to play on first?

80

Playground

Baobab Tree by Andrew Scott

African Portal by Queen Brooks

Thrones to Earth and Sky
by Barbara Chavous

WHAT
DO
YOU
THINK
?

▶ **If you could build a playground, how would you make it different?**

Light and Dark Colors

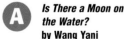

A *Is There a Moon on the Water?*
by Wang Yani

B *Who Picked the Fruit?*
by Wang Yani

C *The Ripe Fruit*
by Wang Yani

Where do you see light browns? Dark browns? Artists add white or black to make a color lighter or darker.

82

A color in nature can be light
or dark, too.

In the Studio

Paint something you would see
outside. Use only green, black,
and white paint. Make dark and
light greens for variety.

Seascapes

A *Rowing Homeward*
by Winslow Homer, 1890

B *The Gulf Stream*
by Winslow Homer, 1889

What is the first thing you see in picture **A**? Picture **B**? The part of an artwork the artist wants you to notice most is called the **emphasis**.

In the Studio

Paint yourself in a seascape.

1. Think about things you see near the sea.

2. Show the water and the sky in your picture.

3. Add yourself to your picture.

MARC

Look at these pictures Marc Brown drew for his book *D.W. All Wet*. What can you tell about the story?

BROWN

The art in a picture book helps tell the story.

Marc Brown

WHAT DO **YOU** THINK ?

▶ Do you think Marc Brown likes his job? Why?

Monoprints to Share

Geraniums
by Bianca Gilchrist, 1991

This artist made a nature painting.

Then she made a **monoprint**.

Mono means "one." There is only one print of the painting.

88

In the Studio

Make a monoprint.

1. Fingerpaint a picture on wax paper.

2. Press a sheet of paper gently onto the wet paint.

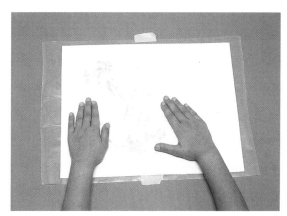

3. Peel the monoprint off the wax paper.

Work slowly!

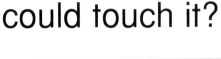

Textures in Clay

How would this jar feel if you could touch it?

B Student artwork

A *Seed Jar*
by Thomas Polacca, 1991

These artworks are made of **clay**. Moist clay is soft and can be shaped. What textures do you see in the clay? How do you think the artist made them?

In the Studio

Make a flat clay animal. Add textures.

1. Make a flat piece of clay into the shape of an animal.

2. Find objects to make textures.

3. Press the objects into the clay.

Feel the textures you made.

Tell us what you saw
on the way to town.
Tell us what you saw
walking up and down.

Mediterranean Scene by Raoul Dufy

What would you see if you were walking around inside this picture?

Two Cheeseburgers with Everything by Claes Oldenburg, 1962

Artful Celebrations

I rarely have soup when
  I'm eating at noon:
It runs through my fork and
  spills out of my spoon!
I'd rather have something
  to eat with my hands,
Like hot dogs and french fries
  or pizza in pans!

—Ruth I. Dowell

ABOUT CLAES OLDENBURG

Claes Oldenburg turns everyday objects into art. He has made artworks of french fries, hot dogs, and baked potatoes!

Lesson 25

USING FOUND OBJECTS

Surprising Sculptures

This artwork can move! What did the artist use to make it? This is a **sculpture**, an artwork you can look at from all sides.

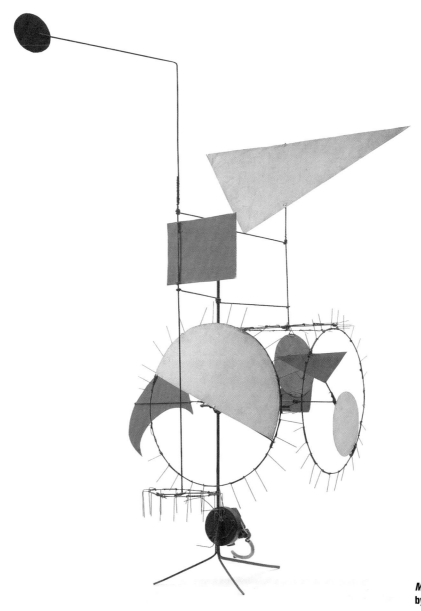

Méta-mécanique
by Jean Tinguely, 1955

In the Studio

Make a sculpture.
Use found objects.

1. Find objects that someone might throw away.

2. Decide how your sculpture will look.

3. Use glue or string to put the objects together.

Sculptures of People

Which of these sculptures do you like best? Why?

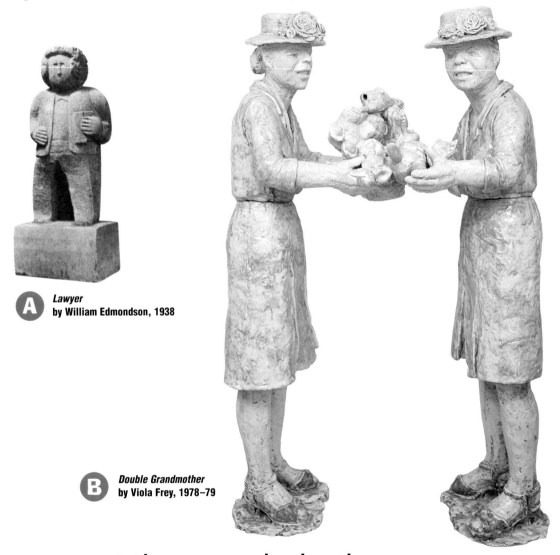

A *Lawyer*
by William Edmondson, 1938

B *Double Grandmother*
by Viola Frey, 1978–79

If you met the people in these sculptures, what stories might they tell?

98

In the Studio

Make a sculpture of a person.

1. Make forms for each part of the person.

2. Put the forms together. Use a little water when you join the pieces.

3. Add details. Let your sculpture dry.

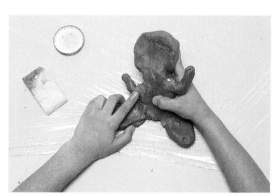

PHOTOGRAPHER Flor Garduño

Some artists tell stories about people by taking pictures of them. Flor Garduño took these photographs in Mexico.

Flor Garduño

King of Canes

Tell a story about this photograph.

Basket of Light

WHAT
DO
YOU
THINK
?

▶ **How is a photograph different from a painting? How are they the same?**

STILL LIFE

Name the things you see in this **still life** painting. A still life shows things that people like to see or use. It can tell you about the artist who painted it.

How Beautiful Life Is When It Gives Us Riches
by Frida Kahlo, 1943

I have these things at home.

In the Studio

Draw a still life.

1. Look at a group of objects.

2. Draw the group of objects in your own way.

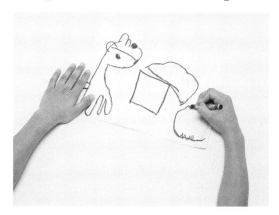

3. Compare your drawing to others. Look for ways each is different.

Quilts

A Baltimore Album Quilt

B Broken Star Quilt, Amish

Look at all the patterns!

Which quilt would you like on your bed? Many quilts tell stories with patterns and pictures. What does picture **A** tell a story about?

In the Studio

Make a square for a quilt.

1. Make sketches of things that stand for the United States.

2. Draw your picture or design on a paper square.

3. Help put the squares together in a class quilt.

PARADES

Art can be for special times, such as a parade. What parades have you seen?

Where do you see art in these pictures?

WHAT DO **YOU** THINK **?**

▶ If you had a parade, what would it be for? What would people see if they watched your parade?

Flags for All

What does this flag mean to you?

Flag
by Jasper Johns, 1954

This art sure looks like a real flag!

In **flags**, shapes and colors stand for important ideas. What shapes and colors are used in many of these flags?

In the Studio

Make a school flag. Use shapes and colors in a design that tells about your school.

American Buildings

Buildings can be art, too. What lines, shapes, and forms do you see in these buildings? People who design buildings are called architects.

A St. Nicholas Orthodox Church, Juneau, Alaska

B The United States Pavilion at Expo '67 by Buckminster Fuller

In the Studio

Make a model of a building.

1. Sketch a building you want to build.

2. Use forms to make the parts of your building.

3. Put the parts of your building together.

Untitled by Keith Haring, 1987

What name would you give this artwork?

Mother's Quilt by Faith Ringgold, ©1983

The World of Art

Gifts of rings and patchwork,

Coins and recipes,

Pumpkin pies and lullabies,

Will bind our families.

— from *Family Gifts*

ABOUT FAITH RINGGOLD

Faith Ringgold is an American artist and writer. She makes quilts with stories and pictures on them. This artist shares her life with us through her quilts.

Playful Puppets

A **puppet** can be a work of art. Artists from many countries make puppets. Puppets are fun to watch, and they can tell important stories. What stories have you seen puppets tell?

Punch, 1820s

In the Studio

Make a sock puppet.

1. Stuff paper into a sock.

2. Use rubber bands to make a head and arms.

3. Add details with paper, yarn, or cloth.

What shapes and patterns do you see?

A *Untitled (Buffalo Architectural Themes)* by Joyce Kozloff, 1984

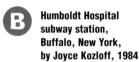
B Humboldt Hospital subway station, Buffalo, New York, by Joyce Kozloff, 1984

This artwork is in a subway station. It is a **mosaic**. A mosaic is a picture made up of small tiles. How did the artist plan her mosaic?

In the Studio

Make a mosaic that shows your favorite shape.

1. Cut or tear colored paper into small pieces.

2. Draw a shape you like.

3. Glue the paper pieces inside and outside the shape.

PIÑATAS

All cultures have special ways of celebrating. At Christmas-time in Mexico, children break open piñatas. Then treats fall like rain!

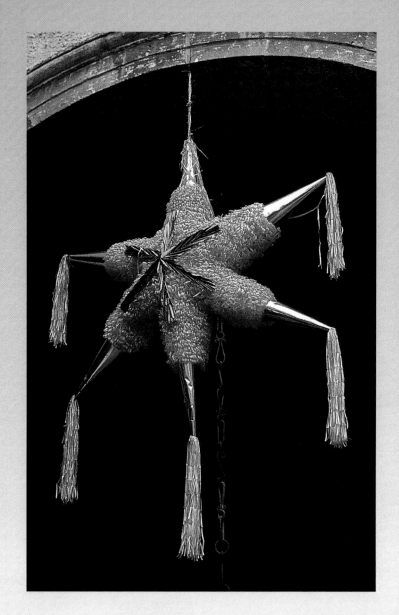

Piñatas are made from clay or paper. They are beautiful to look at but more fun to break. Why?

WHAT DO **YOU** THINK ?

▶ Which piñata do you think is the prettiest? What is your favorite holiday tradition?

121

Lesson
33
PAPER VEST

Clothing

Which of these clothes would you like to wear?

A Silver coin vests, Hmong

B Futurist vest by Fortunato Depero

C Woman's robe (Kosode), late 17th century

An artist puts together the parts of an artwork to make a **design**. Tell about the balance you see in these designs.

122

In the Studio

Make a paper vest that tells about you.

1. Sketch a design on the front of a cut-out vest.

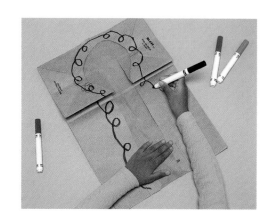

2. Use markers and cloth to add pictures of favorite things.

3. Share your vest with others.

Lesson 34 Jewelry

What patterns do you see?

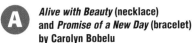

A *Alive with Beauty* (necklace) and *Promise of a New Day* (bracelet) by Carolyn Bobelu

B Star-shaped brooch, 14th century

Jewelry is art that people wear. People around the world make jewelry. Some is for every day, and some is for special times. What kind of jewelry do you like?

In the Studio

Make jewelry that shows a pattern.

1. **Cut different colors of paper into strips.**

2. **Put glue on one side of a strip. Roll the strip around a pencil to make a bead.**

3. **String your beads. Then tie the ends of the string.**

> Roll the paper as tightly as you can.

CONNECTIONS ART AND CULTURE

KITES

It's fun to fly a kite. But some kites are more than toys. They can have beautiful designs.

How are the kites in the pictures the same? How are they different?

WHAT
DO
YOU
THINK
?

▶ **Why do you think kites need large, colorful designs? What design would you like to see on a kite?**

127

PAPER FOLDING

How do you think these artworks were made? Tell about the shapes you see.

A **Drinking birds**

Long ago, artists in Japan started folding paper to make artworks. Which objects do you think were hardest to make? Why?

B Merry-go-round with panda, pig, jumping frog, and Chinese duck

128

In the Studio

Make paper-fan flowers.

1. Fold the paper into a fan.

2. Color a design on the folds of the paper.

3. Open the fan to make a flower. Staple it to a pipe-cleaner stem.

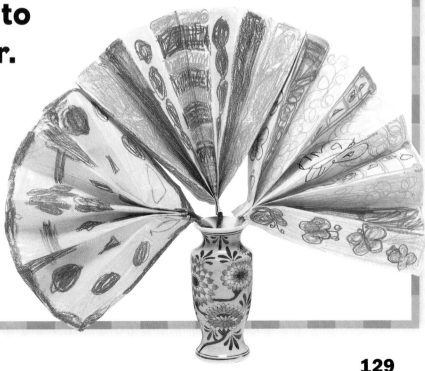

Weaving

How are these baskets the same?
All of these baskets were made by
Native American artists. Why do you
think the design in these baskets
is called the friendship design?

A
Tohono O'odham miniature horsehair
baskets by Norma Antone

B
Tohono O'odham basket with "friendship design"
by Mary Thomas

In the Studio

Weave a place mat.

1. Weave paper strips in and out of a sheet of cut paper.

2. Cut a shape into a folded sheet of paper.

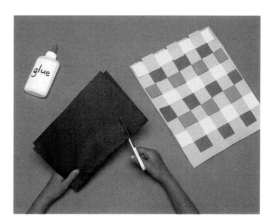

3. Glue the border onto the weave. Add designs with a crayon.

Push the strips together after you weave them.

131

Dance in the circle,
dance in the ring;
Dance in the morning
to welcome the spring.

Spanish Dancers and Cowboy by E. Boyd, about 1820

Why might the dancers be dancing?

ELEMENTS & PRINCIPLES

When you make art, where do you get your ideas? Do you think of a story to tell?

Maybe you want to show your feelings about something.

How do you get started?

Maybe you choose the colors and the tools you will use. These pages tell about the tools artists use to make art.

137

Line

thick

straight

dotted

thin

zigzag

wavy

curved

138

Texture

soft

smooth

furry

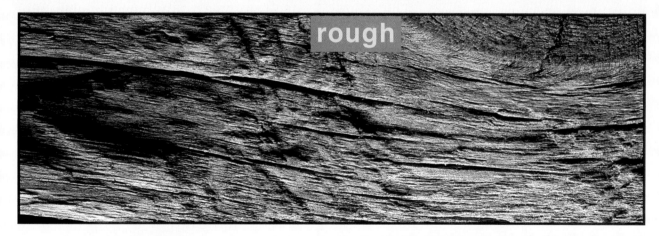

rough

hard

bumpy

Shape

circle

triangle

oval

rectangle

symbols and letters

תאם

تمهّل

S L O W

square

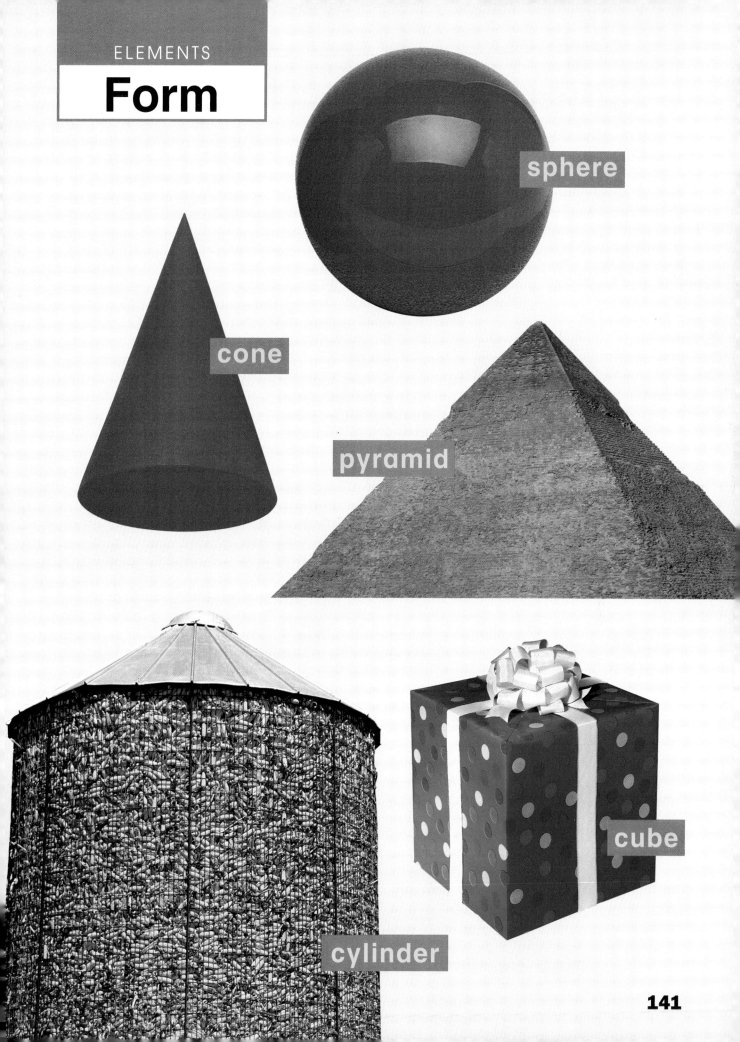

sphere

cone

pyramid

cylinder

cube

ELEMENTS
Color

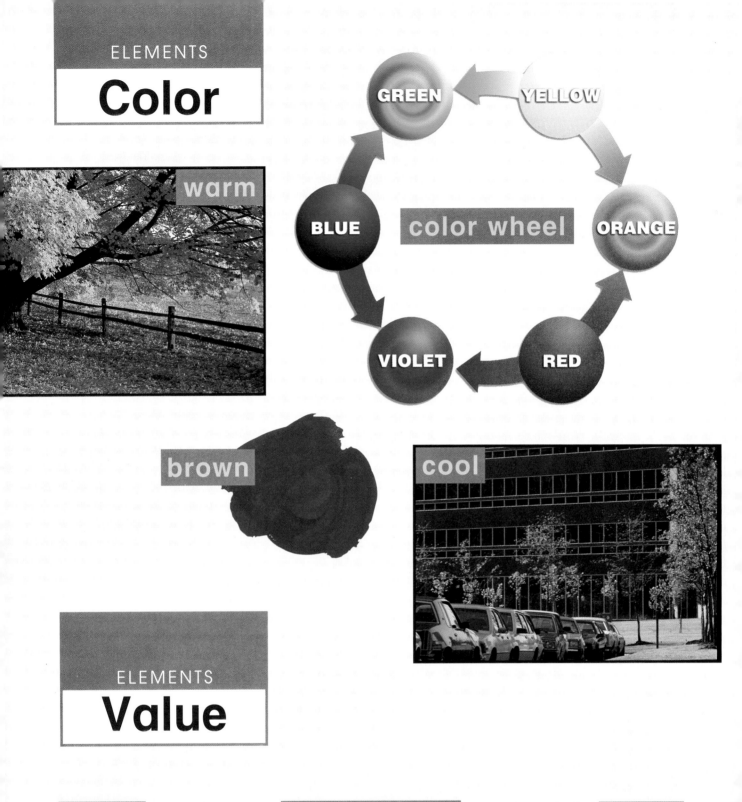

warm

color wheel

GREEN YELLOW BLUE ORANGE VIOLET RED

brown cool

ELEMENTS
Value

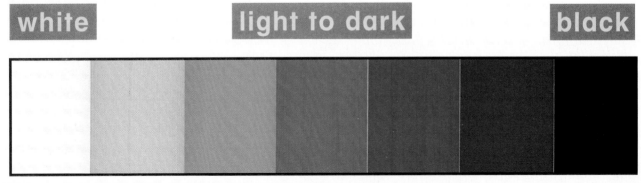

white light to dark black

background

middle ground

foreground

horizon line

143

Unity

repeated lines, textures, colors, shapes, forms

Variety

assorted lines, textures, colors, shapes, forms

PRINCIPLES

Emphasis

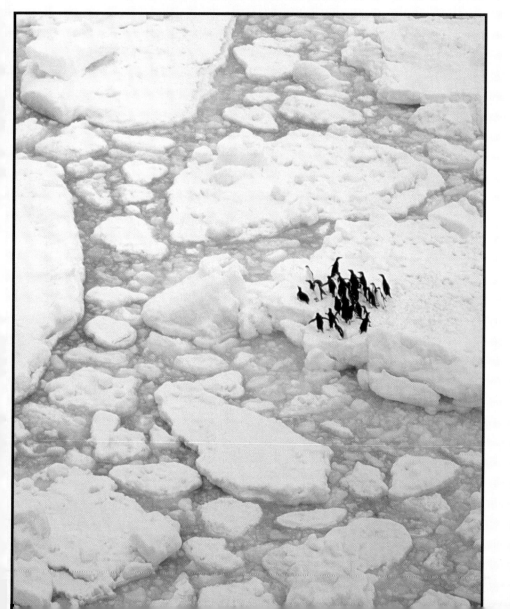

145

146

Movement and Rhythm

Balance

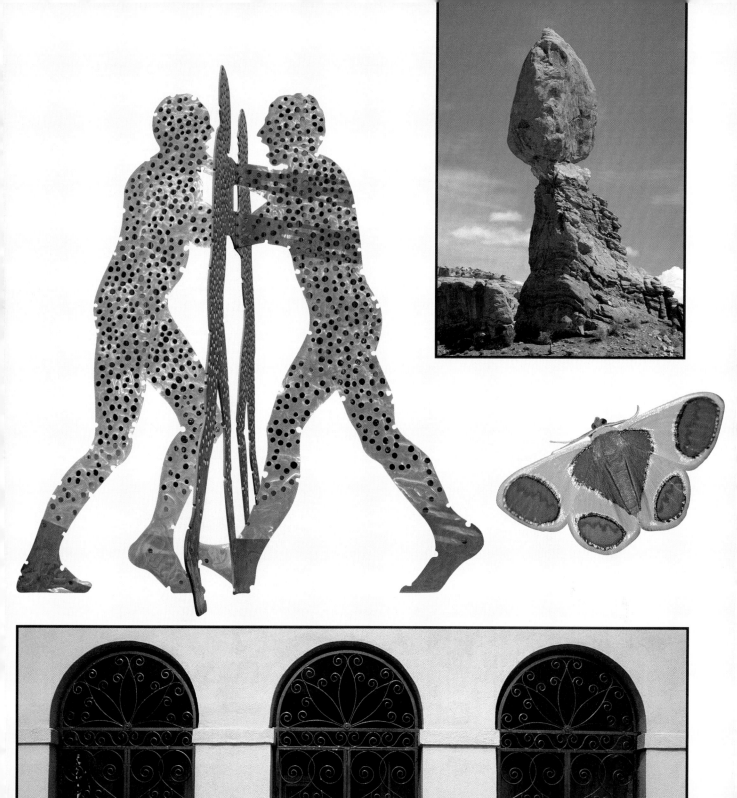

GALLERY OF ARTISTS

Norma Antone

page 130

Carolyn Bobelu

page 124

Romare Bearden (1914–1988)

page 76

Shirley Bowen

page 80

Charles Bell (1935–)

page 70

Queen Brooks

page 80

Marc Brown (1946–)
page 87

Larry Winston Collins
page 80

Eric Carle (1929–)
page 14

Salvador Dalí (1904–1989)
page 18

Barbara Chavous
page 80

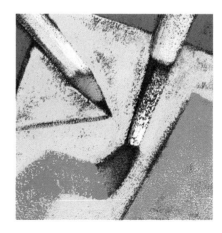

Fortunato Depero (1860–1947)
page 122

Raoul Dufy (1877–1953)

page 92

Gilda M. Edwards (1955–)

page 30

Albrecht Dürer (1471–1528)

page 18

Lois Ehlert (1934–)

page 61

William Edmondson (1870–1951)

page 98

Amos Ferguson (1922–)

page 17

Viola Frey (1933–)
page 98

Flor Garduño (1957–)
page 100

Zeny Fuentes
page 68

Carmen Lomas Garza (1948–)
page 35

Buckminster Fuller (1895–1981)
page 110

Bianca Gilchrist
page 88

Byron Gin (1959–)

page 78

Red Grooms (1937–)

page 24

Grandma Moses (1860–1961)

page 54

Keith Haring (1958–1990)

page 113

Tana Hoban

page 46

David Hockney (1937–)

page 48

Winslow Homer (1836–1910)
page 84

Malvin Gray Johnson
(1896–1934)
page 50

Edward Hopper (1882–1967)
page 25

Frida Kahlo (1907–1954)
page 102

Jasper Johns (1930–)
page 108

Wassily Kandinsky (1866–1944)
page 28

Paul Klee (1879–1940)

page 38

Jacob Lawrence (1917–)

page 42

Joyce Kozloff (1942–)

page 118

Doris Lee (1905–1983)

page 53

John La Farge (1835–1910)

pages 56 and 57

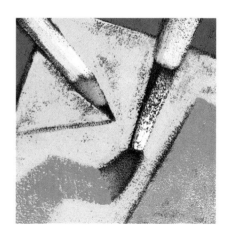

Franz Marc (1880–1916)

page 44

Henri Matisse (1869–1954)
page 36

Pablo Picasso (1881–1973)
page 33

Georgia O'Keeffe (1887–1986)
pages 16, 62, and 73

Thomas Polacca
page 90

Claes Oldenburg (1929–)
page 94

Beatrix Potter (1866–1943)
page 12

George A. Reid (1860–1947)
page 63

Henri Rousseau (1844–1910)
page 74

Germaine Richier (1904–1959)
page 38

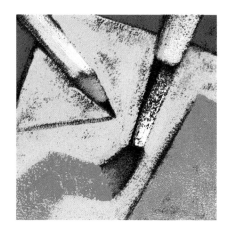

Andrew Scott
page 81

Faith Ringgold (1930–)
page 114

Wayne Thiebaud (1920–)
page 22

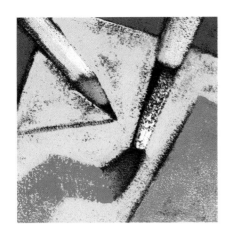

Mary Thomas

page 130

Jean Tinguely (1925–1992)

page 96

Joaquín Torres-García
(1874–1949)

page 79

Marie-Louise-Élisabeth Vigée-
Lebrun (1755–1842)

page 50

Anna Belle Lee Washington
(1924–)

page 64

Wang Yani (1975–)

page 82

GLOSSARY

architect
A person who designs buildings. (page 110)

artist
Someone who makes art. (page 16)

assemblage
An artwork that is made with scraps, found objects, or things from nature. (page 31)

balance
An artwork shows balance when it looks the same on both sides. (page 58)

cityscape

An artwork that shows a city.
(page 78)

clay

Soft material that can be shaped.
(page 90)

collage

An artwork made by gluing pieces
of paper or other things onto paper.
(page 76)

colors

Red, orange, yellow, green, blue,
violet. (page 44)

color wheel

A chart that shows how colors
can be mixed to make new colors.
(page 45)

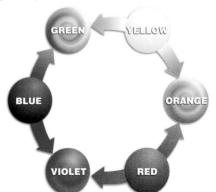

161

cool colors
Colors that seem cool, such as blues and greens. (page 62)

crayon rubbing
A kind of art that shows the texture of an object. (page 49)

curved lines
Lines that are not straight. (page 36)

dark colors
Colors made by adding black to them. (page 82)

details
Small parts of an artwork. (page 70)

design
A plan for the way an artwork will look. (page 122)

drawing

Making a picture of something using lines. (page 17)

emphasis

The part of an artwork you see first. (page 84)

flag

A symbol that stands for a country. (page 108)

form

A shape you can see from all sides. (page 68)

found objects

Things in nature or things that would be thrown away that can be used to make art. (page 97)

horizon line

The place in a picture where land or water and sky meet. (page 64)

jewelry

Art that people wear, usually made of gold or silver and gemstones. (page 124)

landscape

An artwork that shows the outdoors. (page 64)

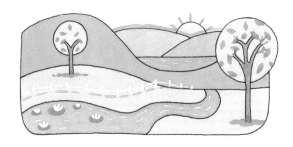

light colors

Colors made by adding white to them. (page 82)

line

A mark that connects two places. (page 36)

mask

A covering for the face. (page 58)

model

A small artwork of something bigger. (page 111)

monoprint

One print made by pressing a clean sheet of paper onto a wet painting and then lifting the paper. (page 88)

mosaic

An artwork made with small pieces of tile, glass, stone, or paper. (page 118)

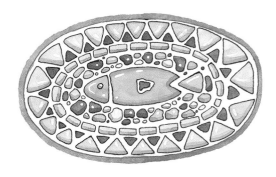

mural

A large painting usually done on a wall. (page 26)

museum

A place that displays artworks. (page 20)

paintbrush

A tool for putting paint on something. (page 29)

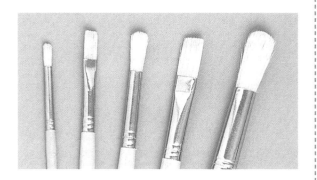

pattern

Lines, shapes, or colors that are repeated. (page 42)

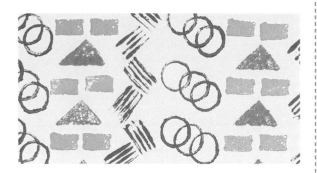

photograph

A picture made with a camera. (page 100)

print

An artwork made by pressing paint on paper with an object. (page 43)

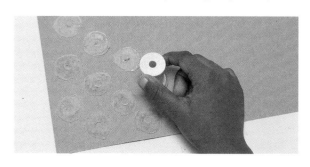

puppet

A small figure made to move with a hand, strings, or rods. (page 116)

quilt

A blanket made from pieces of cloth sewn together. (page 104)

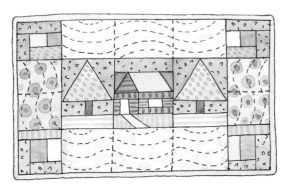

sculpture

An artwork that can be looked at from all sides. (page 96)

seascape

An artwork that shows a lake or the sea. (page 84)

self-portrait

An artist's picture of himself or herself. (page 50)

senses

The way we see, smell, hear, taste, and feel things. (page 22)

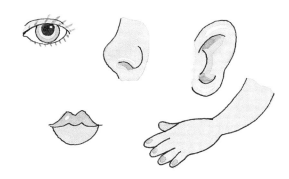

shape

A flat space that is closed by a line. Circles and squares are shapes. (page 38)

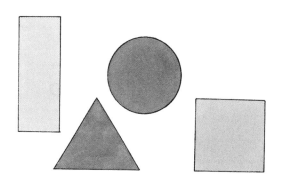

sketchbook

A book in which artists sketch their ideas or things they see. (page 12)

still life

A group of objects arranged by an artist and then shown in an artwork. (page 102)

straight lines

Lines that are not curved. (page 36)

texture

The way something feels or looks as if it feels. (page 48)

unity

An artwork shows unity when all parts look as if they belong together. (page 56)

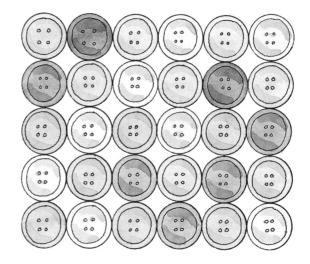

variety

Many colors, shapes, or kinds of lines. (page 76)

warm colors

Colors that seem warm, such as reds and yellows. (page 62)

weaving

Putting threads or strips of paper or cloth over and under one another. (page 130)

zigzag lines

Lines that move up and down. (page 36)

ARTISTS & ARTWORKS

Norma Antone *Tohono O'odham baskets* 130

Romare Bearden *Jazz Village* 76

Charles Bell *Skate* 70

Carolyn Bobelu *Alive with Beauty* 124, *Promise of a New Day* 124

Shirley Bowen African Tell-A-Story Board 80

E. Boyd *Spanish Dancers and Cowboy* 132

Queen Brooks African Portal 81

Barbara Chavous *Thrones to Earth and Sky* 81

Larry Winston Collins African Tell-A-Story Board 80

Salvador Dalí The Space Elephant 18

Fortunato Depero Futurist vest 122

Raoul Dufy *Mediterranean Scene* 92

Albrecht Dürer *The Hare* 18

William Edmondson *Lawyer* 98

Gilda M. Edwards *Mother and Child* 30

Amos Ferguson *The Tree* 17

Viola Frey *Double Grandmother* 98

Zeny Fuentes *Zoo Animals* 68

Buckminster Fuller *The United States Pavilion at Expo '67* 110

Flor Garduño *King of Canes* 100, *Basket of Light* 101

Carmen Lomas Garza *Making Tamales/La Tamalada* 34

Bianca Gilchrist *Geraniums* 88

Byron Gin *Untitled* 78

Red Grooms *Looking along Broadway towards Grace Church* 24

Keith Haring *Untitled* 112

Tana Hoban *photographs* 46

David Hockney *Flowers, Apple & Pear on a Table, July, 1986* 48

Winslow Homer *The Gulf Stream* 84, *Rowing Homeward* 84

Edward Hopper *Rooms by the Sea* 25

Jasper Johns *Flag* 108

Malvin Gray Johnson *Self Portrait* 50

Frida Kahlo *How Beautiful Life Is When It Gives Us Riches* 102

Wassily Kandinsky *Around the Circle* 28

Paul Klee *Senecio* 38

Joyce Kozloff *Untitled (Buffalo Architectural Themes)* 118

John La Farge *Nine-Paneled Firescreen* 56, *Peacocks and Peonies I* 57

Jacob Lawrence *Vaudeville* 42

Doris Lee *Thanksgiving* 52

Franz Marc *Die grossen blauen Pferde (The Large Blue Horses)* 44

Henri Matisse *Red Interior, Still-life on a Blue Table* 36

Grandma (Anna Mary Robertson) Moses *Hoosick Valley (from the Window)* 54

Georgia O'Keeffe *The Lawrence Tree* 16, *From the Plains II* 62, *Autumn Leaves, Lake George, N.Y.* 73

Claes Oldenburg *Two Cheeseburgers with Everything* 94

Pablo Picasso *Three Musicians* 33

Thomas Polacca *Seed Jar* 90

George Agnew Reid *The Northern Entrance to Orient Bay, Lake Nipigon* 63

Germaine Richier *Le Griffu* 38

Faith Ringgold *Mother's Quilt* 114

Henri Rousseau *Exotic Landscape* 74

Andrew Scott *Baobab Tree* 81

Wayne Thiebaud *Pie Counter* 22

Mary Thomas *Tohono O'odham baskets* 130

Jean Tinguely *Méta-mécanique* 96

Joaquín Torres-García *New York City—Bird's Eye View* 79

Marie-Louise-Élisabeth Vigée-Lebrun *Self-portrait* 50

Anna Belle Lee Washington *Day at the Beach* 64

Wang Yani *Is There a Moon on the Water?* 82, *The Ripe Fruit* 82, *Who Picked the Fruit?* 82

INDEX

A

Activities
See Production activities.
Architect, 110, 160
Art and Culture
kites, 126–127
visiting a museum, 20–21
Art and Literature
Brown, Marc, 86–87
Carle, Eric, 14–15
Ehlert, Lois, 60–61
Artists
See Gallery of Artists, 150–159;
Artists and Artworks, 170–171.
Artworks
See Artists and Artworks,
170–171.
Assemblage, 31, 160

B

Balance, 58–59, 122,
148–149, 160
Brooks, Gwendolyn
"Rudolph Is Tired of the City," 55
Brown, Marc
D.W. All Wet, 86–87
Brushstrokes, 29

C

Careers in Art
illustrator, 60–61, 86–87
photographer, 100–101
toy maker, 40–41

Carle, Eric
Draw Me a Star, 14–15
Celebration Art
parades, 106–107
piñatas, 120–121
Cityscapes, 78–79, 161
Clay, 69, 90–91, 161
Clothing as art, 122–123
Collage, 22–23, 76–77, 161
Color, 161
cool/warm, 62–63, 162, 169
light/dark, 82–83, 142, 162, 164
mixing, 44–45
and pattern, 42–43, 56–57
Color wheel, 45, 161
Crayon rubbing, 49, 162

D

Design, 122–123, 162
Details, 70–71, 162

E

Ehlert, Lois
Snowballs, 60–61
Elements of art
color, 44–45, 56–57, 62–63,
82–83, 108–109, 142
form, 68–69, 141
line, 28–29, 36–37, 38–39, 138
shape, 28–29, 38–39, 49, 68–69,
109, 140
texture, 48, 90–91, 139
value, 142
Elements and Principles, 136–149
See also Elements of art,
Principles of design.

Emphasis, 84–85, 145, 163
Everyday Art, 46–47, 66–67

F

Fingerpainting, 89
Flags, 108–109, 163
Form, 68–69, 141, 163
Found objects, 97, 163

H

Horizon line, 64–65, 164

I

In the Studio
    See Production activities.

J

Jewelry, 124–125, 164

K

Keeping a Sketchbook,
    12–13

L

Landscape, 64–65, 164
Line, 28–29, 36–37, 38–39, 138,
    162, 164, 168, 169
Literature
    D.W. All Wet, Marc Brown, 86–87
    Draw Me a Star, Eric Carle, 14–15

"I Rarely Have Soup," Ruth I.
    Dowell, 95
"Rudolph Is Tired of the City,"
    Gwendolyn Brooks, 55
Snowballs, Lois Ehlert, 60–61
"The Very Nicest Place,"
    Anonymous, 35
"Three Little Monkeys,"
    Anonymous, 75
Looking at Art, 10–11

M

Masks, 58–59, 165
Model, 111, 165
Monoprints, 88–89, 165
Mosaics, 118–119, 165
Murals, 26–27, 165
Museum, 20–21, 165

P

Paper folding, 128–129
Pattern, 42–43, 56–57, 124–125,
    146–147, 166
Photograph, 100–101, 166
Postage stamps, 66–67
Potter, Beatrix, 12–13
Principles of design
    balance, 58–59, 122, 148–149
    emphasis, 84–85, 145
    pattern, 42–43, 56–57, 124–125,
        146–147
    unity, 56–57, 144
    variety, 76–77, 144
Printmaking, 43, 88–89
Production activities
    drawing, 17, 19, 25, 37, 57, 71,
        103
    folding paper flowers, 129
    keeping a sketchbook, 12–13

making an animal mask, 59
making an assemblage, 31
making a collage, 23, 77
making a crayon rubbing, 49
making jewelry, 125
making a model of a building, 111
making a mosaic, 119
making paper beads, 125
making a paper vest, 123
making a print, 43, 89
making a quilt square, 105
making a school flag, 109
making a sculpture, 97, 99
making a shape picture, 39
making a sock puppet, 117
painting, 29, 45, 51, 63, 65, 79,
83, 85
using clay, 69, 91
using pipe cleaners, 39
weaving a place mat, 131
Puppets, 116–117, 166

Q

Quilts, 104–105, 166

R

Review, 32, 52, 72, 92, 112, 132
Rhythm, 147

S

Safety, 134–135
Sculpture, 96–97, 98–99, 167
Seascapes, 84–85, 167

Self-portrait, 50–51, 167
Senses, 22, 167
Shape, 29, 38–39, 68–69, 109, 140,
168
Sketchbook, 12–13, 168
Songs
"Dance in the Circle,"
132
"Family Gifts," 115
"Follow Me," 112–113
"The More We Get Together," 52
"Step in Time," 32
"What Have You Seen?" 92
"Windy Weather," 73
Stamps
See Postage stamps.
Still life, 102–103, 168
Symbols, 108–109

T

Texture, 48–49, 90–91, 139, 168

U

Unity, 56–57, 144, 168

V

Value, 142
Variety, 76–77, 144, 169
Viewing, 10–11

W

Weaving, 130–131, 169

ACKNOWLEDGMENTS

PHOTO CREDITS:
Page Placement Key: (t)-top (c)-center (b)-bottom (r)-right (l)-left

Front and Back Cover:
Christian Pierre/Superstock

Table of Contents
Harcourt Brace & Company Photos
4 (tl); 5 (bl), (tr), (cr); 6 (bl); 7 (tr); 8 (cl), (br); Weronica Ankarorn.

Other
4 (br) © 1997 Red Grooms/Artists Rights Society, Courtesy, Marlborough Gallery, NY; 5 (tc) Giraudon/Art Resource; (br) National Museum of American Art, Washington/Art Resource; 6 (tl) Lynton Gardiner/American Museum of Natural History (br) Wally Emerson; 7 (bl) Dale Seymour Pubications; (br) Yale University Art Gallery, Gift of Collection Societe Anonyme; 8 (bl) Woodward & Greenstein American Antiques; 9 (tr) The Metropolitan Museum of Art, Mary Livingston Griggs and Mary Griggs Burke Foundation Gift, 1980; (br) Art Resource.

Frontmatter
Harcourt Brace & Company
10,11 (c) Richard Nowitz; 13 (b) Britt Runion.

Other
12 (l) Rough study for Peter and Benjamin on the wall. Copyright © Frederick Warnes & Co., 1987; (tr) The Granger Collection, New York; (br) Illustration for p23 of "The Tale of Benjamin Bunny," copyright © Frederick Warne & Company, 1904, 1987; 13 (t) The Montessori Community School.

Unit 01
Harcourt Brace & Company
15 (br), 17 (b) 19, 23, 29 (b), 31, Weronica Ankarorn; 32, 33 (br) Britt Runion.

Other
14,15 Illustration by Eric Carle reprinted by permission of Philomel Books from DRAW ME A STAR by Eric Carle, Copyright © 1992 by Eric Carle; (br) Sigrid Estrada; 16 © 1998 The Georgia O'Keeffe Foundation/Artists Rights Society (ARS) New York, Malcolm Varon, NYC © 1997; 17 (t) Amos Ferguson; 18 (l) Descharnes and Descharnes, 18 (r) Planet Art; 20 Robert Frerck/The Stock Market; 21 Mugshots/The Stock Market; 22 (c) Purchase, with funds from the Larry Aldrich Foundation Fund/Whitney Museum of American Art; 24 © 1997 Red Grooms/Artists Rights Society, Courtesy, Marlborough Gallery, NY; 25 (t) Michael Agee/ Yale University Art Gallery, Bequest of Steven Carlton Clark, B. A. 1903; 26, 27 Jim Prigoff; 28 Solomon R. Guggenheim Museum; 29 (t) Crayola Dream-Makers Art Collection, reprinted with permission of Binney & Smith, Inc. The Big Fish and His New Friends by Kristyn Snyder, age 6, Hiram W. Dodd Elementary, Allentown, PA.; 30 Gilda M. Edwards; 33 (t) The Museum of Modern Art, New York, © 1998 Estate of Pablo Picasso/Artists Rights Society (ARS), New York.

Unit 02
Harcourt Brace & Company
37, 39, 43, 45 (bl), 48 (bl), 49, 51, Weronica Ankarorn; 52 (bl),53 (tr), (br) Britt Runion.

Other
34-35 Reprinted with permission of Children's Book Press, San Francisco, Ca.; 36 (tl) John Neubauer/PhotoEdit; (bl) John Neubauer/PhotoEdit; (r) Bridgeman/Art Resource © 1998 Succession H. Matisse, Paris/Artists Rights Society (ARS), New York; 38 (l) Scala/Art Resource, NY; (r) Giraudon/Art Resource, NY; 40, 41 Copyright © 1993 by Ken Heyman. By permission of Lothrop, Lee & Shepard Books, a division of William Morrow & Company, Inc.; 42 (l) Children's Art Exchange; (r) Hirshhorn Museum and Sculpture Garden Smithsonian Institution. Gift of Joseph H. Hirshhorn, 1966. Photography by Lee Stalsworth; 44 (c) Gift of the T. B. Walker Foundation, Gilbert N. Walker Fund/ Walker Art Center, 1942; 46 (b) Photographed by Tana Hoban for her book Shapes, Shapes, Shapes, Copyright © 1986 by Tana Hoban. By permission of Greenwillow Books, a division of William Morrow & Company, Inc.; 47 (l) Charles Philip/Westlight; (ct) Michael Furman Bugatti/The Stock Market; (tr) Swarthout/The Stock Market; (cb) Pedro Coll/The Stock Market; (br) Chris Rogers/The Stock Market; 48 (tl) R. Andrew Odum/Peter Arnold; (br) Collection: David Hockney; 50 (l) Galleria degli Uffizi, Florence/Art Resource; (r) National Museum of American Art, Washington/Art Resource; 52, 53 (c) Mr. and Mrs. Frank G. Logan Prize Fund, 1935 © 1992/The Art Institute of Chicago.

Unit 03
Harcourt Brace & Company
56 (l), 57 (b), 59 Weronica Ankarorn; 60, 61; 65, 68 (r), 69, 71 Weronica Ankarorn; 72 Britt Runion.

Other
54-55 Grandma Moses: Hoosick Valley (From The Window). Copyright © Grandma Moses Properties Co. New York; 55 (br) Cornell Capa/Magnum Photos; 56 (r) The Chrysler Museum of Art, Norfolk, VA, Gift of Walter P. Chrysler, Jr. 74.26.1 Photo By Scott Wolff; 57 (t) National Museum of American Art, Washington DC/Art Resource, NY; 58 (tl) Lynton Gardiner/American Museum of Natural History; (bl) Lynton Gardiner/American Museum of Natural History; (r) Gilbert Graham; 62 © 1998 The Georgia O'Keeffe Foundation/Artists Rights Society (ARS) New York, © Malcolm Varon, NYC; 63 (t) Government of Ontario Art Collection, Toronto/Tom Moore Photography, Toronto; 64 (l) Superstock; (r) Children's Art Exchange; 66 (tr) Nawrocki Stock Photo; (bl) US Post Office; (br) Richard Abarno/The Stock Market; 67 (l) Peter Beck/The Stock Market; (r) Tom McCarthy/PhotoEdit; 68 (tl), (bl), (bc), Wally Emerson; 70 Louis K. Meisel Gallery; 73 © Columbus Museum of Art, Ohio; Museum Purchase: Howald Fund ll.

Unit 04
Harcourt Brace & Company 77, 79 (b) Weronica Ankarorn; 84 (br) Britt Runion; 85, 89, 91 Weronica Ankarorn; 92 (bl), (br), 93 (tr), (br) Britt Runion.

Other
74-75 The Norton Simon Foundation, Pasadena, Ca.; 75 (br) Giraudon/Art Resource; 76 © Romare Howard Bearden Foundation/Licensed by VAGA, New York, NY; 78 Byron Gin/StockWorks; 79 (t) Yale University Art Gallery. Gift of Collection Societe Anonyme.; 80, 81 Debi Drew; 82 Zheng Zhensun; 83 (tl) Anna E. Zuckerman/PhotoEdit; (bl) Alan Oddie/PhotoEdit; (r) Dennis MacDonald/PhotoEdit; 84 (t) Phillips Collection, Washington, D.C./Superstock; (c) Photograph ©1995, The Art Institute of Chicago, All Rights Reserved; 86, 87 From D. W. All Wet by Marc Brown. Copyright © 1988 by Marc Brown. By permission of Little, Brown and Company; 90 (l) Lynn Wallace/Inter-Tribal Indian Ceremonial Association; (r) Dale Seymour Publications; 92- 93 (t) Galerie Fanny Guillon-Laffaille © 1998 Artists Rights Society (ARS), New York/ ADAGP, Paris.

Unit 05
Harcourt Brace & Company 97, 99, 103, 105, 109 (t), 111 Weronica Ankarorn; 112 (bl), 113 (cr) Britt Runion.

Other
94, 95 The Museum of Modern Art, New York. Philip Johnson Fund. Photograph © 1998 The Museum of Modern Art, New York.; (br) Gianfranco Gorgoni/Woodfin Camp & Associates; 96 Foto by Christian Baur, Basel © 1998 Artists Rights Society (ARS), New York/ ADAGP, Paris; (c) Museum Jean Tinguely Basel; 98 (r) The Minneapolis Institute of Arts; 100 (bl) Flor Garduno; 101 Flor Garduno; 102 Collection Francisco and Laura Osio, Photo courtesy The Bronx Museum of the Arts; 104 (tl) Abby Aldrich Rockerfeller Folk Art Center, Williamsburg, Va.; (br) Woodard & Greenstein American Antiques; 106 (l) Joseph Sohm/The Stock Market; (tr) Alan Schein/The Stock Market; (br) David Young-Wolff/PhotoEdit; 107 (t) Stephen McBrady/PhotoEdit; (b) David Young-Wolff/PhotoEdit; 108 (t) The Museum of Modern Art, New York. Gift of Philip Johnson in honor of Alfred H. Barr, Jr. Photograph © 1997 The Museum of Modern Art © 1998/Licensed by VAGA, New York, NY; 108 (b), 109 (b) From The World Book Encyclopedia © 1997 World Book, Inc. By permission of the publisher; 110 (l) Mark E. Gibson/Corbis; (r) Marilyn Silverstone/Magnum Photos; 112, 113 © Keith Haring Foundation.

Unit 06
Harcourt Brace & Company
117, 119, 123, 125, 129, 131, Weronica Ankarorn; 132 (bl), 132,133 border Britt Runion.

Other
114 © 1983 Faith Ringgold, Inc.; 115 Faith Ringgold, Inc.; 116 Smithsonian Institution; 118 (t) Albright-Knox Art Gallery Buffalo, New York Charles W. Goodyear Fund, 1984; (b) Jamie Stillings; 120 Tony Freeman/PhotoEdit; 121 Superstock; 122 (l) Libraries Unlimited; (br) The Metropolitan Museum of Art, Mary Livingston Griggs and Mary Griggs Burke Foundation Gift, 1980 (1980.222); 124 (l) Jerry Jacka Photography; (r) Art Resource; 126 Superstock; 127 (l) David Barnes/The Stock Market; (r) Uniphoto; 128 (l) Nancy Palubniak/Palubniak Studios; (r) By permission of Florence Temko, author of

"Paper Pandas and Jumping Frogs", published by China Books, San Francisco; 130 Jerry Jacka Photography; 132 (c) Photo by:Dean Beasom/National Gallery of Art.

Art Safety
Harcourt Brace & Company
134 (tl), (tr), (bl), (br), 135 (tl), (tr), (br) Terry Sinclair; 135 (bl) Weronica Ankarorn;

Elements and Principles
Harcourt Brace & Company
138 (tc); 139 (br) Earl Kogler; 140 (cr) Victoria Bowen; 141 (cl); 163 (tl), (br), (cr), 164 (bl), (br), 165 (cl), 166 (l), (bl), (cl), 169 (tr) Weronica Ankarorn.

Other
136 (cl) Gene Ahrens/Bruce Coleman, Inc.; (tr) Pete Saloutos/The Stock Market; (b) J.H. Carmichael, Jr./The Image Bank; (cr) W. Geiersperger/The Stock Market; 137
(tl) Gary Withey/Bruce Coleman, Inc.; (tr) Viviane Moos/The Stock Market; (c) Jeffry Myers/The Stock Market; (bl) Antonio M. Rosario/The Image Bank; (br) Lewis Portnoy/The Stock Market; 138 (tl) Walter Bibikow/The Image Bank; (tc) Doug Plummer/Photo Researchers; (tr) Vince Streano/The Stock Market; (cl) Tim Davis/Photo Researchers; (c) Rick Gayle/The Stock Market; (cr) Frank P. Rossotto/The Stock Market; (bl) Andrea Brizzi/The Stock Market; (br) Grafton Marshall Smith/The Stock Market; 139 (tl) Nicolas Russell/The Image Bank; (tr) Zefa Germany/The Stock Market; (bl) Russell D. Curtis/Photo Researchers; 140 (tl) Ed Bock/The Stock Market; (tr) David Parker/SPL/Photo Researchers; (bl) Murray Alcosser/The Image Bank; (br) Lance Nelson/The Stock Market; (cl) Chromosohm/Sohm/Photo Researchers; 141 (t) Garry Gay/The Image Bank; (bl) B. Seitz/Photo Researchers; (br) Chris Collins/The Stock Market; (cr) Raga/The Stock Market; 142 (t) David W. Hamilton/The Image Bank; (b) Schneps/The Image Bank; 143 (t) Patricio Robles Gil/Bruce Coleman, Inc.; (bl) Goblet Philippe/Photo Researchers; (br) Brad Simmons/Bruce Coleman, Inc.; 144 (t) Michael P. Gadomski/Bruce Coleman, Inc.; (bl) Garry Gay/The Image Bank; (bl) Jeff Hunter/The Image Bank; (cl) Marc Romanelli/The Image Bank; (cr) Jim Corwin/Photo Researchers; 145 (tl) Jane Burton/Bruce Coleman, Inc.; (tr) Zefa Germany/The Stock Market; (c) Kenneth W. Fink/Photo Researchers; (bl) Zefa Germany/Bruce Coleman, Inc.; 146 (tr) Linda Albrizio/The Stock Market; (bl) Bob Abraham/The Stock Market; (br) Zefa Germany/The Stock Market; (cl) Randy Duchaine/The Stock Market; 147 (t) Kevin Horan/Tony Stone Images; (c) Geoff Dore/Tony Stone Images; (br) Jeff Spielman/The Image Bank; (bc) David Sailors/The Stock Market; (bl) David Hall/Photo Researchers;148 (b) Strauss/Curtis/The Stock Market; (tr) Harvey Lloyd/The Stock Market; (cr) Alan L. Detrick/Photo Researchers; (cl) Arthur Beck/The Stock Market; 149 (c) Kjellk B. Sandved/Photo Researchers; (b) Brownie Harris/The Stock Market; (tl) Alon Reininger/The Stock Market; (tr) Charlie Or/Photo Researchers.

Gallery of Artists by Artist's last name:
Romare Bearden: Frank Stewart, Charles Bell: Louis K. Meisel Gallery, Queen Brooks: Debbie Drew, Shirley Bowen: Debbie Drew, Marc Brown: Marc Brown, Eric Carle: Sigrid Estrada, Barbara Chavous: Debbie Drew, Larry Collins: Debbie Drew, Salvador Dali: UPI/Corbis-Bettman, Raoul Dufy: © 1997 Artists Rights Society (ARS), New York/ADAGP, ParisGiraudon/Art Resource, Albrecht Durer: Scala/Art Resource, William Edmonson: William Edmondson in Profile by Louise Dahl-Wolfe, gelatin silverprint, 64.3.3, Gift of Louise Dahl-Wolfe Collection, Cheekwood Museum of Art, Gilda Edwards: Tracey Jollay, Lois Elhert: Lillian Schultz, Amos Ferguson: Karen R. Preuss/Dr. Sukie Miller, Goya Francisco: Art Resource, Viola Frey: Jim Arkatov/Nancy Hoffman Gallery, Zeny Fuentes: Wally Emerson, Buckminister Fuller: Yousuf Karsh/Woodfin Camp & Associates, Inc., Flor Garduno: Vilma Slomp, Carmen Lomas Garza: Bob Hsiang, Byron Gin: Stockworks, Red Grooms: Charles Moore/ Black Star, Grandma Moses: Cornell Capa/Magnum Photos, Keith Haring: Patrick Piel/Gamma Liaison, David Hockney: Woodfin Camp & Associates, Inc., Winslow Homer: Corbis-Bettman, Edward Hopper: Pach/Corbis/Bettman, Jasper Johns: Dan Budnik/Woodfin Camp & Associates, Inc., Malvin Gray Johnson: National Museum of American Art: Washington/Art Resource, Frida Kahlo: Schalkwijk/Art Resource, Wassily Kandinsky: The Granger Collection: New York, Paul Klee: Corbis-Bettman, Joyce Kozloff: Kenna Love, John LaFarge: Corbis Bettman, Jacob Lawrence: Eden Arts, Henri Matisse/ Henri Cartier-Bresson/Magnum, Georgia O'Keefe: Dennis Brack/Black Star,Claes Oldenburg: Wide World Pictures, Pablo Picasso: © 1997 Estate of Pablo Picasso/Artists Rights Society (ARS), New York/Giraudon/Art Resouse, NY, Thomas Polacca: Jerry Jacka, Beatrice Potter: The Granger Collection, New York, Faith Ringgold: Wide World Photos, Henri Rousseau: Art Resource, Wayne Thiebaud: Matt Bult, Jean Tinguely: Rene Burri/Magnum Photos, Joaquin Torres-Garcia: Courtesy of Cecilia de Torres, Ltd. New York, Vincent van Gogh: Erich Lessing/Art Resource, Marie-Louise-Elizabeth Vigee-LeBrun: Galleria degli Uffizi: Florence/Art Resource, Anna Belle Lee Washington: Anna Belle Lee Washington, Wang Yani: From "A Young Painter: The Life and Paintings of Wang Yani" by Zheng Zhensun, and Alice Low. © 1991 New China Pictures Company

Glossary
Harcourt Brace & Company
163 (tl), (br), (cr), 164 (bl), (br), 165 (cl), 166 (tl), (tr), (bl), (cl), 169 (tr), Weronica Ankarorn.

Other
160 (tl) Peter Beck/The Stock Market; 164 (tl) Bryan Peterson/The Stock Market; (tr) Steve Elmore/The Stock Market; 165 (br) Claudia Parks/The Stock Market; 166 (cr) David Young-Wolff/PhotoEdit; 168 (tr) Bonnie Kamin/PhotoEdit; 169 (tl) Michele Burgess/The Stock Market.